inside
SHIPS
& subs

inside
SHIPS
& subs

By Steve Parker
Illustrated by Alex Pang

Miles Kelly

First published in 2009 by Miles Kelly Publishing Ltd
Harding's Barn, Bardfield End Green, Thaxted, Essex, CM6 3PX, UK

This edition printed in 2012

©2012 Discovery Communications, LLC. Discovery Explore Your
World™ and the Discovery Explore Your World™ logo are trademarks
of Discovery Communications, LLC, used under license.
All rights reserved. www.yourdiscovery.com

10 9 8 7 6 5 4 3 2 1

Publishing Director: *Belinda Gallagher*
Creative Director: *Jo Cowan*
Design Concept: *Simon Lee*
Volume Design: *Rocket Design*
Cover Designer: *Simon Lee*
Indexer: *Gill Lee*
Production Manager: *Elizabeth Collins*
Reprographics: *Stephan Davis, Thom Allaway*
Consultants: *John and Sue Becklake*
Edition Editor: *Amanda Askew*

ISBN 978-1-84810-831-8

Printed in China

British Library Cataloguing-in-Publication Data
A catalogue record for this book is available from the British Library

Every effort has been made to acknowledge the source and copyright
holder of each picture. Miles Kelly Publishing apologises for any
unintentional errors or omissions.

MADE WITH PAPER FROM
A SUSTAINABLE FOREST

ACKNOWLEDGEMENTS

All panel artworks by Rocket Design
The publishers would like to thank the following
sources for the use of their photographs:
Corbis: 27 Paul A. Souders
Fotolia: 6(b) Alexander Rochau; 7(b) Snowshill;
9 Forgiss; 11 linous; 33 Aaron Kohr
Rex Features: 15 Stuart Clarke; 21 Sipa Press; 23;
31 Sipa Press; 37 c.W. Disney/Everett
Photo Library: 7(c) Bernard van Dierendonck
Science Photo Library: 34 Alexis Rosenfeld
Shutterstock: COVER Atlaspix; 13 pjmorley;
16; 18 Ralf Siemieniec; 29 Sascha Burkard
All other photographs are from Miles Kelly Archives

WWW.FACTSFORPROJECTS.COM

Each top right-hand page directs
you to the Internet to help you
find out more. You can log on
to **www.factsforprojects.com**
to find free pictures, additional
information, videos, fun activities
and further web links. These
are for your own personal use
and should not be copied or
distributed for any commercial
or profit-related purpose.

If you do decide to use the
Internet with your book, here's a
list of what you'll need:
• A PC with Microsoft® Windows®
  XP or later versions, or a
  Macintosh with OS X or later,
  and 512Mb RAM

• A browser such as Microsoft®
  Internet Explorer 9, Firefox 4.X
  or Safari 5.X
• Connection to the Internet.
  Broadband connection
  recommended.
• An account with an Internet
  Service Provider (ISP)
• A sound card for listening to
  sound files

Links won't work?
www.factsforprojects.com is
regularly checked to make sure
the links provide you with lots
of information. Sometimes you
may receive a message saying
that a site is unavailable. If this
happens, just try again later.

Stay safe!
When using the Internet, make
sure you follow these guidelines:
• Ask a parent's or a guardian's
  permission before you log on.
• Never give out your personal
  details, such as your name,
  address or email.
• If a site asks you to log in or
  register by typing your name
  or email address, speak to your
  parent or guardian first.
• If you do receive an email from
  someone you don't know, tell
  an adult and do not reply to the
  message.
• Never arrange to meet anyone
  you have talked to on the
  Internet.

Miles Kelly Publishing is not
responsible for the accuracy or
suitability of the information on
any website other than its own.
We recommend that children are
supervised while on the Internet
and that they do not use Internet
chat rooms.

www.mileskelly.net
info@mileskelly.net

CONTENTS

INTRODUCTION

The first people who sat on a floating fallen tree, then tied a few trimmed tree trunks together as a raft, and then hollowed out one log as a canoe – started something incredible. Thousands of years before cars and aircraft, early traders transported valuable cargoes along rivers and coasts, while explorers crossed oceans to settle new lands. Towns grew up along shorelines, and water became the the most important way to travel.

Kayakers use a double-ended paddle to propel, steer and stop, for complete craft control.

3. When the weight of displaced water equals the weight of the boat, the boat floats

Boat

1. Boat pushes aside or displaces a certain volume of water

Water

2. Displaced water causes an upthrust, or buoyancy, force

SINK OR FLOAT?

The scientific reason why boats float was worked out by Archimedes of ancient Greece. An object lowered into water pushes aside, or displaces, a volume of water. The water pushes back with a force, upthrust, equal to the weight of water displaced. When the object is low enough, the upthrust of the displaced water equals its own weight, and it floats. A heavy stone's weight is always more than the weight of water it displaces, so stones sink.

PADDLES AND SAILS

To sail where you want, you need propulsion. Push against water and it partly pushes back, and human hands were the first true paddles. Larger surfaces for pushing came with paddles and oars, but they were tiring to use. Sails appeared more than 5000 years ago to catch wind power. Oars were still needed because the sail design for travelling into the wind, or tacking, did not arrive for another 4000 years.

Tall ships are traditionally-rigged sailing vessels that are still hugely popular today.

The watercraft featured in this book are Internet linked.
Visit www.factsforprojects.com to find out more.

PROPS ARE TOPS

Steam engines that powered the Industrial Revolution in the late 18th and early 19th centuries soon found their way onto ships. The paddlewheels of early steamers were adapted from the waterwheel familiar at the time. Several inventors experimented with designs of propellers, also called water-screws, which were a reverse version of the Archimedes screw used for moving water. In 1845 the British Navy raced the paddlewheeler *Alecto* against the screw-driven *Rattler*. The latter won easily, and from that time, props were tops.

Rotating prop shaft turns propeller

Thrust bearing

Propeller

Prop shaft to engine

Thrust

Watertight bearing

Rotating prop 'screws' forwards through the water, pushing it back with great force

Section through prop blade

The helmsperson may steer a ship, but the captain is in complete command on the bridge.

Motorcruisers are travelling personal hotels with all mod cons.

BIGGER AND FASTER

Many new kinds of watercraft continued to develop, such as commercial oil supertankers from the 1860s and military aircraft carriers from the 1920s. For fun we have luxury motorcruisers and offshore powerboats for the rich, and jetskis and sailing dinghies for the not-so-rich. Seafaring is easier when a ship's control room, or bridge, bristles with the latest gadgets such as radar, sonar, satellite weather maps and GPS satnav.

As fuel prices rise, sail power could return in earnest – but heavy seas, high tides, and unpredictable currents and storms will still challenge the most experienced sailors well into the future.

YACHT

For more than 5000 years, starting along the river Nile in ancient Egypt, people used the wind to push their ships and boats along. Boats propelled by oars go back farther still, but sailing is easier than rowing – provided there is some wind. Yachts are mainly fairly small, light sailing craft. They are used for fun and pleasure, or for racing, rather than for carrying big loads of cargo.

One of the world's largest sailing yachts is Maltese Falcon, with masts 58 m tall, 15 sails and a length of 88 m – as long as a soccer pitch.

Eureka!

Until about 1100 years ago sailing ships had mainly square sails that could only be pushed by the wind. Then the lanteen, or triangular sail, was invented, which could be swung around to catch the wind from any angle.

Whatever next?

Modern energy costs are high, but wind power is free. Boat designers are testing big cargo-carrying ships with both engines and sails.

Mast Tall upright poles, or spars, are masts. They hold up the tops of the sails and keep the vertical sides straight.

✳ How do SAILS work?

The boom holds the sail at an angle to the wind so that the wind pushes it along, partly forwards and partly sideways. The boat does not slide sideways because of its hull shape and the large surface area of the keel or centreboard, which both resist sideways movement. The sail also forms a curved shape, like an aircraft wing. Air passes over the curve more quickly than under it (see page 19) to 'suck' the boat along.

In 1989, 77-year-old Tawny Pupot sailed across the Atlantic Ocean single-handed in 72 days.

Jib

Deck

Keel

Wind pressure causes the boat to lean to the side

Sail

Wind

Hull

Boat is pushed forwards

The keel resists the sideways force created by the wind blowing onto the sail, this forces the boat forwards

Take a guided tour of one the biggest and most luxurious yachts by visiting www.factsforprojects.com and clicking on the web link.

Sails Some yachts have one sail, others 20 or more. They are made from very strong tear-proof fabric, either natural fibres such as cotton or flax (linen), or artificial fibres like nylon and polyester.

The ships with the biggest sails were 'clippers' bringing tea and spices from East Asia to Europe and North America. The famous Cutty Sark was launched in 1869. It had more than 30 sails with a total area of almost 3000 square metres – bigger than ten tennis courts.

Boom The pole or tube forming the boom is attached along the bottom, or foot, of the sail. It can swing the sail around according to the wind direction.

Main sail

Rigging Various kinds of ropes, or lines, hold up the mast (standing rigging) and move the sails (running rigging). They are made from strong, smooth-running, rot-proof fibres and steel rope.

Windsurfers can reach speeds of 90 km/h

Frames and bulkheads U-shaped frames give the hull (the main body of the boat) its strength and form, and have holes to save weight. Bulkheads are like dividing walls inside the hull.

SAILBOARDING

In 1948 Newman Darby fixed a sail and a mast mounted on a swivel joint onto a small, flat-bottomed boat and invented the sailboard. The rider holds a double-sided boom and tilts the sail to catch the wind, moving along the board and leaning back so that it does not flip over.

RACING CATAMARAN

The 'cat' is a boat with two hulls (main bodies) usually of equal size. It has several advantages over the usual single hull or monohull. For example, it is so wide that it is much more difficult to capsize – tip over onto its side in the water. The hulls, called vakas, are connected by one or more decks, or akas, that hold the masts. Catamarans were used in South Asia for centuries but only became accepted for official racing in the 1970s.

Eureka!

In the 1690s, part-time pirate William Dampier described catamaran-style double-canoes in the Bay of Bengal, in the Indian Ocean. However boat-builders did not start to use the design until Nathanael Herreshoff made a 'cat' in 1876/77.

Since the 1970s, huge engine-powered catamarans have become popular as high-speed ferries carrying people and vehicles, and even huge trucks. They are smoother and safer in rough seas than hydrofoils.

Sails 'Cats' can have a bigger sail area than a monohull boat because they are more steady and stable in the water.

Boom

Wheel

Rails

✳ How do HULLS AND MULTI-HULLS work?

A monohull may tip over if it has heavy loads on deck and tall sails. The deep-keeled monohull is more stable since the keel adds weight low down and its surface area resists tipping. 'Cats' and trimarans (three-hulled craft) have wider bases with a larger deck area for cabins, people and equipment.

Monohull   Monohull with deep keel

Multi-hull Trimaran   Multi-hull Catamaran

Stern This is the rear or 'aft' end of the boat, which usually has the rudder for steering.

Rudder

Keel The keel resists sideways pressure and forces the boat to move forwards.

Watch an exciting video of a catamaran race by visiting www.factsforprojects.com and clicking on the web link.

Alloy mast The mast is made from alloys, or mixtures of metals and other substances, especially aluminium. It is a hollow tube, lighter and stronger than a solid rod.

One of the newest, largest catamarans is Hemisphere, 44 m long and 500 tonnes in weight, with a 52-m-tall mast. It carries 12 guests on luxury cruises around the Caribbean, manned by a crew of eight.

The fastest round-the-world sailing trip was in 2004 by legendary adventurer Steve Fossett and a crew of 12. In their catamaran Cheyenne they took 58 days and nine hours. The record was broken a year later by Bruno Peyron in Orange II, taking 50 days 16 hours.

A catamaran race, with spinnakers rigged

☀ What are SPINNAKERS?

The spinnaker is a large sail that blows out like a balloon. It works like a normal sail when moving in the direction of the wind, or at an angle downwind. However unlike a normal sail, the spinnaker cannot sail into the wind. This means that racing sailors put up, or rig, the spinnaker for the downwind parts of their course, then roll or furl it and use the normal sails for the upwind parts of the race.

Bow This is the front or 'forward' end of the boat, which is sharp and streamlined to slice through the water easily.

Lightweight hull Modern 'cats' have hulls made of very light but strong materials such as fibre-glass or carbon-fibre composites.

JET SKI

The PWC, personal watercraft, is often called a 'jet ski' or 'aquabike'. It's a combination of motorcycle and speedboat, powered by a 'jet' of water that makes the hull 'ski' across the surface. Jet skis are mainly for fun, racing and stunt-riding. However they are also useful for emergencies, such as rescuing a swimmer swept away by strong water currents.

Eureka!

The first jet skis were invented by bank official and off-road motorbike enthusiast Clayton Jacobson in the early 1970s. They were built by Kawasaki, which also makes fast, powerful motorcycles.

Whatever next?

Some jet skis are fitted with a small parachute so that the rider can take off at speed over the crest of a wave, open the parachute to float back down, reel in the parachute quickly, and start all over again.

In 2002, Count Alvaro de Marichalar y Sáenz de Tejada of Spain took four months, riding 12 hours each day, to travel from Rome, Italy across the Mediterranean Sea to Gibraltar and then across the Atlantic Ocean to Miami, USA – all on a jet ski.

Handlebars · Engine · Drive shaft · Impeller · Water is sucked in to the intake · Ducting · Water is forced out of the nozzle at high speed, pushing the jet ski forwards

✳ How does WATERJET PROPULSION work?

The impeller sucks in water from below the craft and forces it out rearwards at high pressure through the nozzle. The force of the water blasting backwards pushes the craft forwards. The nozzle is connected by cables to the handlebars. Turning the handlebars to the left makes the nozzle swing to the left, so the craft steers left. The rider can also steer by 'leaning' the craft as on a motorbike.

Engine Some jet skis have four-stroke petrol engines, others are two-stroke (see page 14). The engine is low down to make the craft stable so it does not tip over.

Front fairing

Rub strip

Hull

Discover everything you need to know about personal watercraft by visiting www.factsforprojects.com and clicking on the web link.

Hinged handlebars On some jet skis the handlebars are part of the main body. On others they are mounted on a hinged upright tube so the rider can stand up as well as sit down.

EXPLODED VIEW

Seat

A jet ski stunt rider gets some 'big air'

Some jet skis reach speeds of more than 100 km/h, and riders have travelled 1000 km in 24 hours.

✳ AQUABATICS!

Jet ski riders don't just race. They also have freestyle competitions for tricks and stunts such as somersaults, backflips, mid-air spins and barrel rolls, and even diving under the surface and surging back up again into the air. The riders earn points for each manoeuvre as well as speed as they race around a track marked by floating buoys.

GL-X900

GL-X

In freeriding, jet ski riders use waves and surf as jump ramps to take off and reach amazing heights.

Drive shaft A long spinning shaft from the engine turns the impeller. The drive shaft has watertight seals around it so water cannot leak into the engine compartment.

The jet ski rider has an ignition key on a rope or line tied to the wrist or lifejacket. The key slots into the ignition switch before the engine can start. If the rider falls off the key comes out and the engine stops.

Impeller Shaped like a fan or propeller, the impeller spins quickly inside its duct (curved tube).

Jet nozzle The jet of water blasts out of a tube-like nozzle to push the jet ski along.

Impeller duct Water is sucked in for the impeller through an opening or inlet. This has a mesh-like grate or screen to keep out larger objects such as seaweed, driftwood and fish.

OUTBOARD SPEEDBOAT

A speedboat has a long, streamlined hull with a sharp front or bow. The lower surface is designed to 'plane' or skim over the surface at high speed. This is faster than a hull that is partially submerged and tries to push or carve through the water. An outboard engine is one mounted outside the main hull, rather than inboard or within the hull.

Eureka!

The hydroplane is a special design of speedboat devised in the 1950s. It has two sponsons, or short projections, one on each side at the front of the hull. These give stability and lift the craft clear of the water except for its propeller.

Whatever next?

In 1978 Ken Warby reached a speed of 510 kilometres per hour in his hydroplane *Spirit of Australia*. Several people have since died trying to break this record.

Dash The dash or control board has dials for information such as engine temperature and fuel level.

Controls The steering wheel is linked by cables to the outboard motor and makes it swivel from side to side.

Until 1911 the world water speed record was held by steam-powered boats.

Fuel tank Fuel for a two-stroke engine has special lubrication oil mixed with the petrol.

Planing shape The hydroplaning hull is almost flat-bottomed or shaped like a shallow V. It lifts nearly clear of the water at high speed, to avoid the water pushing back to cause resistance or drag.

✳ How does a TWO-STROKE ENGINE work?

A two-stroke engine produces power every two strokes of the piston inside the cylinder. The upstroke squashes a mixture of fuel and air in the cylinder above the piston, while sucking fresh fuel-air mixture into the crankcase below the piston. The mixture burns or combusts and forces the piston down. This transfers the fresh fuel-air mixture from below the piston to above, where the fresh mixture also pushes out the burnt mixture.

1. Fuel mixture is compressed and ignited

2. Fresh fuel mixture is sucked into crankcase

3. Combustion forces piston down

4. Compressed fuel mixture is pushed from crankcase to cylinder

5. Burnt mixture is pushed out (exhaust)

Spark plug

Cylinder

Con-rod

Crankcase

Crankshaft

Piston

Side port

Con rod turns crankshaft

Upstroke

Downstroke

Carbon fibre hull The hull must be extremely strong and rigid, for slamming into waves at great speed.

Download a video of Ken Warby setting the world speed record by visiting www.factsforprojects.com and clicking on the web link.

World water speed ace Ken Warby built his craft *Spirit of Australia* at home. He set the world water speed record in 1978 at Blowering Dam, on the Tumut River in the Snowy Mountains of southeast Australia.

A powerboat 'guns' its engines

Seat The pilot's seat is well padded since even small ripples on the surface cause sudden jolts and knocks at speed.

✳ LUXURY POWER

Motorcruisers, motoryachts and similar powerboats are not built for out-and-out speed. However they are great for travelling relatively fast, more than 60 kilometres per hour, and in comfort. Larger versions are equipped with berths (beds), a saloon (living area) and a galley (kitchen). The main control area is the cockpit, and on top of this may be an open area, the flybridge, with a second set of controls for use in good weather.

Rear seat fairing

Engine

Drive shaft

Bevel gearing

Transom

Grab handles

Fuel tank

Rudder

Propeller

In 1980, Lee Taylor tried to break Warby's record at Lake Tahoe, Nevada, USA. His craft *Discovery II* buckled and crashed and he died.

OFFSHORE POWERBOAT

Offshore powerboats are built to withstand waves, wind and weather away from the shore, out in the open ocean. Slamming into a wave at 160 kilometres per hour is almost like hitting a brick wall. Powerboats have to be enormously tough, strong and rigid. They are usually powered by twin marine diesel or petrol engines. In World Championship P1 races, the diesels can be up to 13 litres – six times the size of a family car engine.

Eureka!

The diesel engine was invented by Rudolf Diesel in the early 1890s. It is heavier than a petrol engine but a useful design where much power is needed, as in powerboats, trucks and tractors.

Whatever next?

Electric powerboats have been around since 1880. The latest models can travel faster than 100 kilometres per hour, are quiet and do not produce polluting fumes.

One of the longest offshore powerboat races is the Round Britain competition, which covers 2500 km at average speeds of more than 100 km/h.

Fuel tanks Some powerboats hold well over 1000 litres of fuel, enough for cruising for most of the day.

Hull shape Powerboats 'plane' or skim with only the propellers and rudders under the surface. The hull is made from aluminium-based metal alloys or carbon-fibre composites.

Rails

Cleat

Inner structure Apart from fuel tanks, inside the watertight hull is mostly air, so the boat is very light. The framework of metal alloy keeps the hull shape rigid.

✳ High speed ACTION

Powerboat racing is extremely expensive – a top team needs to spend tens of millions of pounds. However it's not just pure speed that wins. The boats must be reliable and economical with fuel. The pilots, or drivers, have to take into account waves, tides, currents and wind, and keep a constant lookout for dangers such as driftwood. Crashing through the waves is physically demanding, even when strapped into well-padded seats.

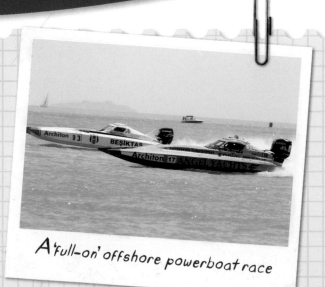

A 'full-on' offshore powerboat race

Some powerboat meetings consist of several races, such as a sprint of less than 50 km and an endurance of more than 150 km.

Read facts, watch videos and download photos of offshore powerboats by visiting www.factsforprojects.com and clicking on the web link.

Air intakes

Aerofoil wing

Windscreen

Rudder The rudder is linked to the steering wheel by cables running along inside the hull. Some boats have two rudders, one near each propeller.

Inboard engines The twin marine diesels are at the rear, under large covers that can be removed to service and repair them.

Engine cooling Marine diesels are cooled by sea water taken in continuously through an inlet and expelled through an outlet, rather than water circulating through a radiator as in a car.

✳ How do DIESEL ENGINES work?

A diesel engine has four stages or strokes:
1. Inlet: The piston moves down and sucks in a mixture of fuel and air. **2. Compression:** The piston moves up and squashes or compresses the mixture. **3. Combustion:** The mixture is so hot from compression it explodes, forcing the piston down. **4. Exhaust:** The piston goes up and pushes out the burnt mixture. The piston's up-down movements turn the engine's main shaft, the crankshaft, by a connecting rod.

Depending on conditions, some powerboats race at more than 250 km/h. However in some events, if the weather is bad, they are kept to lower speeds by a device called a limiter fixed to the engine.

1. Fuel mixture enters cylinder through inlet valve

2. Piston moves up as inlet valve closes

3. Mixture is ignited by high pressure, pushing piston down

4. Piston moves up pushing out burnt mixture

Cylinder

Piston

Con-rod

Crank shaft

Con-rod turns crankshaft

5. Burnt mixture leaves through exhaust valve

6. Con-rod turns crankshaft

Stroke 1

Stroke 2

Stroke 3

Stroke 4

HYDROFOIL

Hydrofoil watercraft 'fly' above the surface on wing-like foils fixed to struts beneath the hull. The foil works like an aircraft wing to generate a lifting force at speed, which raises the foil so the craft above it is above the surface. This greatly reduces the drag or resistance of the craft moving through the water. It also means the hull is held clear of rough water and waves.

Eureka!

Hydrofoils were developed in stages by several scientists and engineers, including John Thornycroft around 1900, Alexander Graham Bell (inventor of the telephone) from about 1906 and Enrico Forlanini in 1910.

Whatever next?

Engineers are always working on new foil designs, including 'smart' foils that can alter their curved shape according to their speed.

The sit-down hydrofoil is like a chair on a large water ski that 'flies' over the water, towed behind a speedboat.

Rails

Bulkheads

Propellers One prop turns faster than the other to steer the craft.

Drive shafts The long drive or propeller shafts extend deep below the boat, so the propellers remain in the water when the hull is lifted clear.

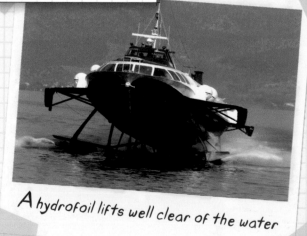

A hydrofoil lifts well clear of the water

✳ HANDY HOPS

Commercial hydrofoils run as fast ferries in many areas, especially South and East Asia. They provide a quick smooth ride, handy for hops across lakes, rivers, bays and sheltered inshore waters. However they may have trouble with large waves and high winds.

Struts The struts are thin with sharp front and rear edges to produce as little water resistance as possible. On some hydrofoils they can swivel left or right to work as rudders.

Learn about jetfoils and how they work by visiting www.factsforprojects.com and clicking on the web link.

Some surfers have boards fitted with foils to cope with really big waves away from the shore.

Water flow is faster over the foil, resulting in lower pressure

Hydrofoil is sucked upwards, supporting the weight of the hull

Strut

Foil shape with curved upper surface

Sea

Trailing edge

Leading edge

Direction of travel

Water flow is slower under the foil, resulting in higher pressure

✳ How do HYDROFOILS work?

A foil's shape is curved when seen edge-on, known as an aerofoil (see page 8). The curve is greater on the upper surface than the lower. Water flowing past the foil must go faster over the top than beneath. Faster water means less water pressure. So the lower pressure above the foil sucks it upwards with a force called lift, raising the hull out of the water.

Seats

Bridge

Among the most successful hydrofoils are the Boeing 929 'Jetfoils'. Some versions can carry more than 200 passengers at a cruising speed of 80 km/h.

Engines Most commercial hydrofoils have one or two diesel engines positioned in the lower hull, for good stability and balance.

Hull The hull gradually rises as the craft picks up speed. It is built from a material such as advanced GRPCFC, glass-fibre-reinforced plastic carbon-fibre composite.

Disco Volante was a fictional hydrofoil in the James Bond adventure 'Thunderball'. It was owned by an agent of Bond's arch enemy organization SPECTRE.

Foils Some foils are shaped like a shallow V while others are like an upside-down T or U. They are made of strong rigid metal.

MILITARY HOVERCRAFT

Hovercrafts fly rather than sail, floating just above the surface. They are also known as ACVs, Air Cushion Vehicles. Their great benefit is that they can travel across smooth ground as well as water. The giant LCAC, Landing Craft Air Cushion, is the US military's combined boat, low-altitude aircraft and load-carrier. It can take troops, vehicles and equipment from a larger transport ship to the shore and even up onto the land.

Eureka!

The first full-sized working hovercraft, SRN-1, was built in 1959 by Christopher Cockerell and his team from the Saunders Roe aircraft makers. It hovered at a height of about 25 centimetres.

Whatever next?

Personal hovercraft are gaining popularity, but mainly for fun and racing. They are not allowed to travel on roads and are awkward to steer in high winds.

LCACs carry a load of 70 tonnes – the weight of an Abrams M1 battle tank.

Bow thruster This tube carries some of the air from the lift fans and can be turned to blow it in any direction to help with manoeuvring and steering.

✳ How do HOVERCRAFTS work?

A hovercraft floats on a high-pressure 'cushion' of air. Its lift fans (impellers) have large angled blades and are driven by an engine such as a gas turbine (as used in helicopters). The lift fan blows air downwards with great speed and force. The air collects in the skirt area below and builds up enough pressure to lift the craft. As the skirt rises, air begins to escape from under its edge but the pressure remains high enough for the craft to hover.

Control station

Ramp

Air is sucked in through intake

Lift fan pushes air down at great speed

Lift fan

Flexible rubber skirt

Sea

High pressure cushion of air builds up in skirt

The US LCAC is almost 25 m long, 14 m wide and 7.2 m high when hovering.

Discover everything you need to know about the amazing LCAC
by visiting www.factsforprojects.com and clicking on the web link.

LIFT FAN

Bow thruster

Rear lift fan

Front lift fan

Air outlet ducting

The British Griffon 2000 TD
hovercraft is in service with
more than seven military forces
around the world.

Propeller The large aircraft-type propeller is housed in a collar-like shroud with the rudder just behind.

Rudder

Prop shaft Each propeller spins on a shaft driven by a gas turbine engine, which produces more than 4500 horsepower.

Engine housing

US NAVY

✱ Get the BALANCE right

A hovercraft must be balanced or trimmed so that the weight of the craft plus its load is evenly spread. If not, it it might hover nose-down rather than level, or lean to one side and veer around. The loadmaster's job is to put all parts of the load into the correct places and secure them for stable balance.

Outlets

Skirt The flexible rubberized skirt hangs down around the hull. It traps air to raise the air pressure and lift the craft and passes easily over waves.

Loading a military hovercraft

EXPLODED VIEW

PASSENGER HOVERCRAFT

Hovercraft that carry passengers and vehicles have been used in many parts of the world, although they are less common today. They can fly off the water up onto a ramp to load and unload. They are also fast, cruising at more than 100 kilometres per hour, and the trip is smooth in calm weather. However the ride is noisy and big waves make the craft sway and rock making some passengers sick.

Eureka!

Early types of hovercraft had no skirts and tipped over easily. The flexible multi-section skirt was developed in 1962 by Denys Bliss, a colleague of Christopher Cockerell, and helped rectify the stability problem.

Whatever next?

A new breed of hovercrafts are exploring remote swamps. They cause little disturbance to wildlife as they switch off their engines and observe rare animals.

Bridge The bridge is the control centre of a large ship, where the captain and pilot or helmsperson keep watch and steer.

Radar

Controls A hovercraft's main controls are the lift throttle or lever to adjust hovering height, main throttle for speed and the steering wheel for the rudders.

The largest commercial hovercraft included the French N500 Naviplane and the British SR-N4. They weighed about 250 tonnes, were 50 m long and could carry 400 passengers and more than 50 cars.

The Russian ZUBR are the largest hovercraft in the world, weighing 550 tonnes – 150 tonnes more than a fully loaded jumbo jet.

Seats

Skirt

Life raft containers

Hovercraft steers left

Propellers push hovercraft forwards

Fast-moving air from the propeller pushes past the rudders

Rudders deflect air to the left

Rudder

✳ How does a HOVERCRAFT STEER?

Like a propeller aircraft, a hovercraft is pushed along by its props. In some versions the propellers swivel left or right on their pylons to blow air at an angle for steering around corners. Other types have rudders that push the air to the side and make the hovercraft turn. Control is tricky in high winds.

Watch a hovercraft in action by visiting
www.factsforprojects.com and clicking on the web link.

The giant SR-N4 hovercraft went into service in 1968 but
was phased out by 2000 due to increasing fuel costs.

Propeller pylon

Propeller The propellers or thrust fans are usually made from advanced composite materials and can spin more than 50 times each second.

Rudder The rudder is directly behind the propeller, where it has most effect in the stream of very fast-moving air.

Engine Smaller hovercraft can be powered by turbocharged diesels, and larger ones by gas turbine engines.

In the mid-1950s, British engineer Christopher Cockerell built a number of ground-effect machine test models.

Steps

Lift fan

In 1716, Emanuel Swedenborg drew the first hovercraft design, but he had no suitable engine so he suggested human-powered oars. It would never have worked!

An artist's impression of the
Boeing GEV

✳ SEA MONSTERS?

A Ground-Effect Vehicle, or ekranoplan, has wings like an aircraft and a hull-shaped body like a boat. As it picks up speed on the water, the angled wings create an air cushion between themselves and the water below that lifts the craft just above the surface. It cannot rise higher because without the ground effect the wings do not produce enough lift. GEVs weighing more than 500 tonnes and cruising at more than 500 kilometres per hour, powered by turbojet engines, have been tested for military use on large lakes and inland seas.

CRUISE LINER

It's a luxury hotel with every comfort, from swimming pools to cinemas, restaurants and gyms – all travelling smoothly across the ocean. Cruise liners are holiday homes to thousands of passengers as they visit famous ports and sightseeing locations. When a liner docks, passengers go off to visit the sights as the crew work fast to restock the ship with food, water, fuel and other essentials.

Eureka!

The first purpose-built cruise liner was *Prinzessin Victoria Louise*, launched in 1900. It weighed 4400 tonnes and travelled across the Atlantic and Caribbean, as well as the Mediterranean and Black seas. When it ran aground in 1906, the captain felt so guilty that he shot himself.

Whatever next?

Vast cruise ships planned for the future may have a grassy central area like a city park with paths, flower borders and trees.

Radar mast

One of the largest cruise ships is Queen Mary 2, launched in 2003. At 150,000 tonnes in weight, it is 344 m in length – longer than three soccer pitches.

Bridge

Bow

A powerful tug helps a cruise liner into port

*Give us a TOW!

It takes several kilometres for a massive ship to slow down and stop. During this time it can be blown off course by winds or carried along by tides and currents. Tugs are small, powerful boats that tow big ships using strong cables called hawsers. They may even 'nudge' the bigger ships. The tug captain knows local conditions well and inches the ship into the correct position. Two or more tugs may work together for extra control.

Cargo hold Stores such as fresh water and food are kept towards the bottom of the hull. They must be tied or lashed down to prevent rolling about or falling over in rough seas. Their weight is ballast to increase the ship's stability.

Discover everything there is to know about cruise liners by
visiting www.factsforprojects.com and clicking on the web link.

Queen Mary 2 carries
3000 passengers and 1250 crew.
Some of the most luxurious ships
have more crew and staff than
passengers.

Funnel

Lifeboats

Pool

Cabins
below waterline

Cabin windows

Column The drive shaft for the propeller in the thruster passes down inside the column or stalk, connected to the engine by gears.

Azimuth thrusters These thrusters push the boat along and also swivel to give it sideways thrust for manoeuvring, so there is no need for a rudder.

Engines The diesel engines, usually two or four, are low down in the ship for stability.

Propellers The propellers are made from metal alloys less affected by corrosive sea water.

Shroud The thrusters have a shroud, like a collar, around the propeller for protection and to direct the water for extra pushing force. Some thruster designs have an open propeller, lacking the shroud.

A ship called
The World has
apartments you
can buy. You can
stay in them for a
time or live there
permanently as
the ship travels
slowly round and
round the globe.

Hull

Propeller drive
shaft inside swivel
mounting

Shroud
or duct

Direction
of spin

Propeller

Thruster turns
to apply force
in any direction

The force created by the
spinning propeller moves the ship

✳ How do BOW THRUSTERS work?

Giant cruise liners often have to enter small ports or harbours. The main rudders do not work at low speed, so there are bow thrusters – as main propellers, or as small extra props at the bow (front) and perhaps stern (rear). They swivel around to produce a push or thrust in any direction. The liner can move sideways, diagonally or backwards.

FREIGHTER

Cargo ships, freighters and other similar ships are the hard-working 'trucks' of the ocean. They criss-cross seas around the world carrying all manner of freight and cargo, from cars and televisions to food and flowers. As soon as they reach a port they unload quickly, fill up with another load and set off once more. Global trade is big business where time is money and cannot be wasted.

Eureka!

Cranes were loading and unloading ships in ancient Greece, more than 2500 years ago. Mathematician and scientist Archimedes (287–212 BC) designed one so huge that it could lift enemy ships out of the water!

Mast

Coasters are ships with a small draught – that is, the hull does not extend very far down into the water. They can travel through shallow water and over rocks and reefs where ocean-going ships with much deeper hulls would run aground.

Bridge The ship is controlled from the bridge, with the wheel for steering, speed controls and displays showing information such as engine temperature, fuel levels and much more.

In 2008, a Japanese cargo ship, able to carry 6400 cars, set sail, powered partly by electricity from more than 320 solar panels.

Rudder

Propeller

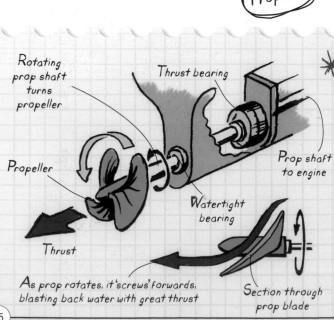

Rotating prop shaft turns propeller

Thrust bearing

Propeller

Prop shaft to engine

Watertight bearing

Thrust

As prop rotates, it 'screws' forwards, blasting back water with great thrust

Section through prop blade

✳ How do WATER SCREWS work?

A water screw or ship's propeller has angled blades that spin around to push the water backwards and so thrust the ship forwards. They are designed with a foil-type shape so that they are sucked forwards as well as pushing backwards (see page 19). The drive shaft or prop shaft from the engine passes through several sets of bearings that transfer the force of thrust from the prop to the ship's hull.

Hull Most working cargo ships have hulls made of steel plates welded together for long-lasting strength and toughness. They can also be repaired easily.

Look at some incredible pictures of huge freighters and bulk carriers
by visiting www.factsforprojects.com and clicking on the web link.

Hook Different-sized hooks can be fitted to the cranes, depending on the loads being lifted.

Grain being piped into the hold
of a large transport ship

*Handling BULK

Some freighters are bulkers or bulk carriers. This means they carry a load that is not made up of large packages or containers, but of gas or liquid, or small, dry solid items such as grains of wheat, sand, cement, small chunks of coal or lumps of metal ore. Grains and powders can be loaded and unloaded along pipes using powerful air suction, like a vacuum cleaner, to make them 'flow'. More lumpy cargoes are lifted out with huge buckets or scoops.

Hatchways These are large openings through which the loads are lowered in and lifted out.

Crane

Transfer pipes

Anchors

Forward hold Holds are storage spaces within the hull. Some go almost to the base or keel of the hull, others have separate layers or decks inside.

Freighters on certain routes cannot be too big, otherwise they would not fit into short-cut canals and locks. The width of the Panama Canal's locks in Central America, is 33.5 m.

Bulbous bow

CONTAINER SHIP

The container ship or 'box boat' carries hundreds of containers in its hold and also stacked in piles on its deck. Standard containers are enormous metal boxes, mostly 12.2 metres long by 2.44 metres wide by 2.59 metres high. They are filled with all kinds of goods and materials, and then transported by road, rail – and ship.

Eureka!

Container ships were first used in the 1950s. The earliest ones were made from converted oil tankers that were built during World War II (1939–1945).

Whatever next?

Containers made out of modern composite materials are more expensive to build, but they are lighter to transport and could pay for themselves in five years.

Dockside cranes Many container ships only have small cranes. They rely mainly on huge purpose-built overhanging cranes that run along rails on the dockside to load and unload their containers.

Bulkheads The strong steel hull has partitions called bulkheads that separate it into watertight compartments. If one is damaged and leaks, the others keep the ship afloat.

Up to 10,000 containers are probably lost at sea each year. Most slip overboard during high winds or storms, while others sink with their ship.

Winch

✳ How do SHIP-BORNE CRANES work?

Many cranes on ships are hydraulic, worked by high-pressure oil. The oil is pumped into a cylinder and pushes along a piston linked by a connecting rod to the crane's 'arm' – the jib or boom. The jib lowers to extend the reach of the crane, and the whole crane swivels around on its base. The cable goes around pulleys or sheaves and is reeled in slowly but powerfully by an electric winch.

Jib

Upper sheaf

Cables

Lower sheaf

Hook

Winch in mast

Swivel joint

Hydraulic pistons move jib up and down

Mast

Load

Cargo too large to carry in containers can be handled using flat racks, open top containers and platforms.

Watch amazing videos of container ships in action by visiting
www.factsforprojects.com and clicking on the web link.

Bridge The captain and crew on the bridge use closed-circuit television, CCTV, with cameras on all parts of the ship to check loading and unloading.

Lifeboats Vessels over a certain size must carry enough lifeboats for all the people on board. The lifeboats must also be checked regularly to make sure they are in good condition and can be launched quickly.

Funnel

EXPLODED VIEW

Engines

Containers stacked up at port

Hold Containers are stacked carefully according to weight, with the heaviest ones lowest down.

Containers Computers are used to plan the order of loading and stacking the containers, so the ship can leave as soon as possible.

A large container ship carries more than 7000 'boxes'.

More than nine-tenths of all the world's cargo (not including bulk materials, see page 26) are transported by containers.

✳ Stack 'em HIGH

Containers slot together so they do not slip or topple. They are weatherproof as they may be stacked at a port for weeks or even months, and they are exposed whilst at sea. The standard 12-metre container weighs about 3.8 tonnes and can hold up to 26.6 tonnes of contents, giving an overall weight of 30.4 tonnes.

OIL SUPERTANKER

The world's biggest ships are the bulk carriers known as oil tankers. Crude carriers transport crude oil, or petroleum, from oilfields such as those in the Middle East to countries all around the world. Product carriers convey the substances made from crude oil at refineries, such as fuels like petrol, diesel and kerosene, lubricating oils, alcohols and chemical solvents.

Eureka!

Oil tankers were first used in the 1860s in eastern Asia, sailing across the Caspian Sea and along the rivers of northern Europe. By the 1890s, tankers were crossing all major oceans.

Whatever next?

The biggest oil tankers are 'sitting duck' targets for pirates, enemies in war, terrorists and other dangers. Some shipbuilders now use smaller, faster carriers to avoid these risks.

A cofferdam is a small space left open between two bulkheads to give protection from heat, fire, or collision. Tankers generally have cofferdams forward and aft of the cargo tanks, and sometimes between individual tanks.

Loading pipes Flexible hoses and rigid pipes carry the pumped oil in and out, and also transfer it between tanks to spread the load for good balance

Supertankers are more accurately known as ULCCs, Ultra Large Crude Carriers, carrying more than 320,000 tonnes of cargo.

Waterline mark

Hull Most modern tankers are double-hulled, with two layers of 'skins' in case one is damaged and leaks. The hard hull surface forms a huge area for reflecting sonar pulses, so other ships can detect the supertanker even at night or in thick fog by sonar as well as radar.

✳ How does SONAR work?

Sonar, Sound Navigation And Ranging, detects nearby objects in water using sound waves. A transmitter sends out pulses or 'pings' that travel far and fast through the water. These bounce off objects as echoes that are detected by a receiver. The direction and timing of the echoes shows the position and distance (range) of the object. Sonar is like a sound version of radar (see page 33).

5. Ship's computer displays information

1. Ship emits sound waves or tows sonar probe

2. Probe emits sound waves

4. Echoes (reflected waves) detected by probe

3. Sound waves bounce off surfaces such as sea bed

Discover everything you need to know about supertankers by visiting www.factsforprojects.com and clicking on the web link.

Pumping control station
Huge pumps driven by electric motors force oil into the hold tanks when loading, and out again at the destination. They are usually sited all together in the pump room.

A large oil tanker starts to slow down at least one hour and 20 km before it needs to stop. In an emergency, it can stop in about 15 minutes and 3 km.

Bridge

Crane

Propeller

Cofferdam

Long hull

Oil tanks As the oil is unloaded and the tanks empty, they are filled with inert gases that do not combine or react with other substances. Otherwise the oil fumes might catch fire and explode.

Bulkheads One vast tank inside the hull would allow oil to slosh around and upset the ship's balance. So bulkhead walls divide it into many compartments.

By weight, oil tankers form more than one-third of all cargo carried at sea.

The world's largest supertanker was Seawise Giant, built in 1979. It was extended, damaged by enemy attack, altered again, and had names including Happy Giant and Jahre Viking. Finally it became the 458-m-long floating oil storage tank Knock Nevis, moored off Qatar in the Middle East.

Oil pollutes the sea from 'Braer' oil tanker off the Scottish coast in 1993

✳ Environmental DISASTERS

Oil tanker accidents have caused some of the greatest environmental disasters of modern times. The oil leaks out as a floating slick that smothers the water's surface and kills fish, seabirds, seals, corals and other marine life. One of the worst spills was in 1991 when the ABT Summer leaked more than a quarter of a million tonnes of oil off Angola, Africa.

AIRCRAFT CARRIER

Some of the largest ships in the world are floating air bases designed to go to anywhere for war – or hopefully, to guard the peace. In addition to carrying jet aircraft and helicopters, these giant vessels have other weapons such as guided missiles, torpedoes and mines. They also act as command, control and communications centres for other seacraft in their fleet such as battleships and destroyers.

Eureka!

In 1910 Eugene Ely was the first pilot to take off from a ship, the US armoured cruiser *Birmingham*. The next year he was first to land on a ship, the USS *Pennsylvania*, another cruiser with a specially built platform.

Whatever next?

Stealth planes scatter radar signals with their angled surfaces, edged shapes and radio-absorbing paint. Stealth ships with similar features have also been tested and will become more common.

Nimitz class carriers have two nuclear reactors powering four steam turbines and can cruise at more than 50 km/h.

✳ How do carriers store AIRCRAFT?

Carriers have huge flat elevators or lifts – platforms that rise up and down between the lower decks and flight deck, transporting aircraft and equipment. Nimitz carriers have four of these along the sides, called upper-stage elevators. They only go down two decks. Then their loads have to be moved sideways to lower-stage elevators inside the hull, which take them down further.

Fuel tanks Huge tanks store jet fuel for the aircraft. Many carriers are nuclear-powered so their plutonium fuel pellets could fit into a small truck.

Flight deck Longer than three soccer pitches, the flight deck is 76 metres wide at its broadest part.

Catapult rail

Island

Flight deck

Crane

Hanger entrance

Aircraft have folding wings to take up less space

Upper stage elevator forms part of flight deck when raised

Anchor

Air defence guns

The flight deck of an aircraft carrier is one of the world's most dangerous places to work.

Hull The steel alloy hull on a US Nimitz class carrier is more than 300 metres long, with a flight deck about 20 metres above the water.

Discover lots more information about aircraft carriers by visiting www.factsforprojects.com and clicking on the web link.

Bridge The bridge (ship's control room), aircraft control centre, radar and radio equipment are in the 'island' on the right or starboard side, leaving the main deck free for planes.

Radar

Aircraft landing

Elevators

Workshops Servicing and repair must be done on the aircraft while at sea, with a full range of parts and spares.

Key carrier crew members include the 'shooter' who oversees the steam-powered aircraft launch catapults, and the handler who controls where aircraft are positioned and stored so that they are available as needed.

Hangars Supercarriers can hold more than 80 aircraft including strike fighter-bombers and slower reconnaissance planes for observing and spying.

✳ The importance of RADAR

Radar (Radio Direction And Ranging) works like sonar (see page 30) but uses radio waves instead of sound. Radar can detect nearby ships, shorelines and hazards such as icebergs showing above the surface, and also aircraft or other objects in the sky many hundreds of kilometres away. Radar cannot be used beneath the surface because radio waves travel very poorly underwater.

Big carriers have a ship's crew of up to 3000 people, and another 3000 aircraft crew including pilots and maintenance engineers.

A complex array of radar and radio masts on a modern carrier

SUBMARINE

A submarine is designed to travel underwater for long distances. (Submersibles go deeper but not long distances, see page 36.) Most large subs are military craft, known as the 'silent service' because they can remain hidden under the surface and undetected for weeks or even months. To do this they must carry all their fuel, food and other stores, although they can make fresh water to drink and also vital oxygen to breathe, both from sea water.

Eureka!

The first submarines were built in the 1620s by Cornelius Drebbel. Powered by oars, they were rowed along the river Thames to impress King James I. In 1776 David Bushnell built the *Turtle*, the first military submarine, to attack British ships in the American War of Independence (1775–1783).

Whatever next?

One of the strangest sports is submarine racing. Spectators try to spot the positions of the submarines by the bubbles they release, or their periscopes – if it ever happens, that is!

Ballistic missile

Periscope The periscope is a vertical telescope that extends from the tower when the sub is 'below' (submerged), to see around at the surface.

Tower The fin, sail or conning (control) tower is where people enter and leave through hatches, and where the crew can keep watch when the sub is at the surface.

Bridge

✳ UNDERSEA WORLD

Many coastal areas now have tourist submarines where visitors can travel beneath the surface to watch fish, corals and other underwater life. It's easier than scuba-diving! The latest versions are 20 metres long, carry 50 passengers down to 100 metres, and stay under for more than an hour. They are powered by electric motors driven by rechargeable batteries so they are quiet and cause almost no pollution.

Bunks

Sonar sphere

In 1958 the US submarine Nautilus sailed past the North Pole – under the floating raft of ice that covers most of the Arctic Ocean.

Tourists enjoy an all-round view

EXPLODED VIEW

Carry out an experiment to discover how submarines dive and rise by visiting www.factsforprojects.com and clicking on the web link.

Most submarines can only descend a few hundred metres at the most. American *Seawolf* subs would probably be crushed below 500 m. The Russian *Komsomlets* sub could reach 1200 m.

Nuclear reactor The nuclear reactor is contained in a radiation-proof casing. In many subs it only needs refuelling every 12–15 years.

Turbines Heat from the nuclear reactor boils water that pushes at huge pressure past the angled blades of a turbine, making it spin to turn the propellers.

Propeller The prop is designed to work very quietly, without forming too many swirls or bubbles, so that other boats cannot hear or see the sub approaching.

Galley

Mess room

726

Planes Hydroplanes tilt to make the submarine rise or fall, and the rudders steer it left or right.

Ballast tanks These chambers are between the outer waterproof hull and the inner pressure hull that withstands the incredible pressure at depth.

Some submarines can stay underwater for more than six months. The limit is not so much fuel, drinking water or oxygen but food for the crew.

Air out
Air in
Ballast tank
Water in
Going down
Water out
Coming up

✳ How do subs WORK?

A sub goes up or down using the ballast tanks between its inner and outer hulls. To sink, it allows air out of the tanks and water in. This makes the sub heavier than the water around it, so it descends. To rise, compressed air made from sea water is forced at high pressure into the tanks. Here the air expands, and although it weighs the same as when compressed, it takes up more space – which was formerly occupied by much heavier water. The sub is now lighter, so it ascends.

DEEP-SEA SUBMERSIBLE

Submersibles are specialized to dive very deep but not travel too far (unlike submarines). They are used mainly for scientific research, surveys and exploring wrecks. Crewed submersibles must have air inside, and the pressure of the water around would crush an ordinary submarine like paper. The best shape to withstand all-around pressure is all round – like the sphere of *Trieste*. In 1960 it descended to Earth's lowest point, the Challenger Deep in the northwest Pacific. No craft or people have ever been nearer to the centre of the Earth.

Eureka!

In 1985 in the north-west Atlantic Ocean the remote submersible Argo, a sled-like design with cameras, located the wreck of the massive liner *Titanic*. It had sunk in 1912 and rested 3800 metres down on the seabed.

Whatever next?

An 'undersea town' where people live and work will allow scientists to study ocean wildlife. They would not have to keep coming up to the surface, which involves slow depressurization to avoid the dangerous condition known as the 'bends'.

Piccard and Walsh spent 20 minutes on the Challenger Deep seabed, eating chocolate for extra energy.

ROVs (Remote Operated Vehicles) are uncrewed submersibles controlled by a long cable, the umbilical or tether. Some have TV cameras and mechanical hands so the operator at the surface can see and hold items.

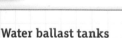
Propeller

Water ballast tanks
The water tanks were positioned at the front and rear of the upper float part.

Gasoline tanks
Filling most of the upper float part, these tanks contained 85 cubic metres of gasoline (petrol).

✳ How did TRIESTE work?

The crew sphere had to withstand pressures of more than one tonne on a fingernail-sized area. Made of 13-centimetre thick steel, it weighed 8 tonnes in water and would sink like a stone. So it was made buoyant by the upper float part containing lighter-than-water gasoline (petrol). The water ballast tanks were adjusted so the craft descended slowly. At the end of the dive, release magnets allowed iron ballast to fall out of the ballast hoppers, making the whole craft lighter so it could rise.

Gasoline filled tanks • Float part of craft • Water ballast tanks • Crew sphere • Trieste's crew sphere was so heavy it would have sunk without the float part • Seabed

Ballast hopper
Nine tonnes of ballast or weight in these two chambers was in the form of small iron pellets.

Release magnets

Discover deep-sea machines, how they work and what they find by visiting www.factsforprojects.com and clicking on the web link.

In 1996 the remote submersible *Kaiko* dived to 10,895 m in the Challenger Deep – not quite as far as *Trieste*.

Entrance hatch The hatch opened into a tunnel that went through the middle of the upper float part of the craft to the crew sphere below.

The crew on *Trieste*'s record-breaking dive were Jacques Piccard, son of the craft's designer Auguste, and Don Walsh.

Snorkel

Tunnel

A *Mir* submersible surveying the wreck of the *Titanic*

✳ Into the DEEP

One of the best-known submersibles is Alvin, launched in 1964 and operated by the US Woods Hole Oceanographic Institution. It can carry three people to depths of more than 4500 metres on trips lasting up to ten hours. In 1977 Alvin was first to discover 'black smoker' deep-sea hot-water vents on the floor of the Pacific Ocean. In 1986 it visited the wreck of the *Titanic* in the Atlantic.

TRIESTE

Fin

Trieste descended about 10,911 m into the Challenger Deep, a narrow gash in the seabed, part of the Mariana Trench. This depth is greater than the height of Mount Everest, at 8848 m.

Crew sphere The two-person crew sat in a hollow steel ball that measured 2.1 metres across.

Window

GLOSSARY

Hydrofoil

Aerofoil

The cross-section shape of most aircraft wings, being more curved or humped on the upper surface than the lower surface, to provide a lifting force. Also the cross-section shape for various water vessel parts such as propellers (water-screws) and the foils of hydrofoils.

Alloy

A combination of metals, or metals and other substances, for special purposes such as great strength, extreme lightness, resistance to high temperatures, or all of these.

Azimuth

To do with angles and movements in the horizontal plane, that is, left and right, level with the water's surface. An azimuth thruster can swivel to point in various directions horizontally, but it cannot tilt vertically to point up or down.

Ballast

Heavy substances, such as water, concrete or metal, added to a craft or vehicle to make it more stable and to stop it toppling over, for example, in high winds or when turning at speed. Many boats and ships have ballast tanks low in the hull that can be flooded with water if the vessel is not loaded heavily enough, so that they float at the correct level and remain steady while moving and turning.

Boom

In watercraft, the pole or spar along the base, or foot, of a sail. It prevents the bottom area of the sail from flapping out of control.

Bow

In watercraft, the front or pointed end of the hull, or main body.

Bridge

In watercraft, the control room of a large boat or ship, housing the wheel (steering wheel), engine throttles, instrument displays and other important equipment.

Bulkhead

An upright wall or partition across the width of a structure, such as across the hull of a ship or the fuselage of an aircraft.

Cleat

A device or structure for attaching lines or ropes, which may be shaped like a cylinder, a 'T', a 'V' or a similar design.

Cofferdam

An empty space between two bulkheads, for ballast or for safety, for example, to stop leakage of dangerous substances into the rest of the vessel.

Sails

Con-rod

Connecting rod, an engine part that links the piston to the main crankshaft.

Crankcase

The main body of a petrol or diesel engine, below the pistons and cylinders, containing the crankshaft and con-rods.

Thruster

Crankshaft

The main turning shaft in an engine, which is made to rotate by the up-and-down movements of the pistons.

Cylinder

In an engine, the chamber inside which a well-fitting piston moves.

Diesel engine

An internal combustion engine (one that burns or combusts fuel inside a chamber, the cylinder), which uses diesel fuel, and causes this to explode by pressure alone rather than by using a spark plug.

Drive shaft

A spinning shaft from an engine or motor that drives or powers another part, such as the propeller of a water vessel.

Hold

In larger ships and boats, the place where cargo, freight and stores are kept.

Hull

The main body or central part of a water vessel.

Hydrofoil

A watercraft that uses wing-like foils to create a lifting force as they move forwards, and so make the hull rise, either partly or completely above the surface.

Impeller

A propeller, rotor or spinning fan inside a tube, collar or shroud, to take in a fluid at one end and force it out at the other end.

Jib

A smallish, usually triangular sail in front of the mainsail(s), towards the front of the vessel. This is also the term used for the working arm of a crane.

Keel

A large flap or flange sticking down below the centre of the hull, with its flat surfaces facing to each side. Keels are used mainly in sailing vessels to give greater control and stability. The term is also used for the central part of a vessel's structure, like its 'backbone' running from front to rear.

Mast

An upright or almost upright pole or spar that holds up and supports one or more sails.

Nozzle

A cone- or trumpet-shaped device from which fast-moving liquid or gas comes out, as in a jetski.

Hovercraft

Petrol engine

An internal combustion engine (one that burns or combusts fuel inside a chamber, the cylinder) that uses petrol fuel and causes this to explode using a spark plug.

Piston

A wide, rod-shaped part, similar in shape to a food or drinks can, that moves along or up and down inside a close-fitting chamber, the cylinder.

Planing (hydroplaning)

In watercraft, moving by skimming over the surface with almost no part in the water, rather than by pushing through it.

Propeller

A spinning device with angled blades, like a rotating fan, which turns to draw in fluid such as water or air at the front, and thrust it powerfully backwards. Also called a water-screw in water vessels or an airscrew in aircraft.

Rigging

Lines (as the ropes are called on ships), masts, sails and other equipment that make a sailing ship travel along under wind power.

Rudder

The control surface of a craft, usually a flat part sticking down below the rear of a boat or ship. It angles to the side to make the craft steer left or right.

Shroud

A collar- or tube-like structure around a spinning impeller (propeller-like fan), which restricts and controls the direction and force of the fluid passing through it.

Stern

In watercraft, the rear or blunt end of the hull, or main body.

Transom

The flat rear panel across some watercraft, which is usually almost vertical and faces backwards.

Throttle

A control that allows more fuel and air into an engine for greater speed, sometimes called an accelerator.

Thruster

A small propeller, nozzle or jet-like part that squirts or puffs out liquid or gas, usually to make small adjustments to a craft's position or its direction of travel.

Turbine

A set of angled fan-like blades on a spinning shaft, used in many areas of engineering, from pumps and cars to boat and jet engines.

Jet ski propulsion

INDEX